Seven Keys to Success, Prosperity and Happiness

Seven Keys to Success, Prosperity and Happiness

A guide to unlocking your potential.

Lyn Genders

ISBN: 1 84013 517 4

Copyright © Axiom Publishing, 2002.

This edition produced for Grange Books
Units 1-6 Kingsnorth Ind. Est.
Hoo, nr Rochester
Kent ME3 9ND
United Kingdom
www.Grangebooks.co.uk

This book is copyright. Apart from any fair dealing for the purpose of private study, research, criticism or review, as permitted under the Copyright Act, no part may be reproduced by any process without written permission. Enquiries should be made to the publisher.

Printed in Malaysia

Grange Books PLC

Contents

Introduction	8

Key No 1   11
Discovering Your Real Needs and Desires
What are your real needs and desires.
Finding your unique talents and true path.
Starting your process of exploration.
Understanding the essence of what you desire.
Giving your desires and ideas time to germinate.

Key No 2   23
Connecting With Your Creative Source
Your Higher Self
Inner guidance and intuition

Key No 3   33
Harnessing and Unleashing Your Creative Power
The process of manifestation
Thoughts
Beliefs
Choices
Taking responsibility for creating your experiences
Life as a mirror
Attitude
Declaring your intention
Affirmation
Resistance to affirmations
Affirmations that communicate confidence
Allowing change

Key No 4
Overcoming Obstacles
70

Gradual journey of discovery and change
Comfort zone
Fear
Feeling and expressing all your emotions
Creating balance and a feeling of wholeness
Masculine and feminine
Giving and receiving
Your relationship with money
Belief in scarcity
Self-sabotage

Key No 5
Fostering An Attitude of Success and Prosperity
93

Honouring your worthiness to receive
Gratitude
Living in the present moment
Releasing

Key No 6
Setting Goals and Taking Action
108

Goals
Goal setting
Reinforce your goals
Action
Acknowledge and celebrate your success

Key No 7   **117**
Persevering and Remaining Determined (Yet Flexible)
   Optimism and perseverance
   Faith, trust and expectation
   Patience
   Detachment

The Next Step   **124**
   From Creator to Co-Creator

Recommended Reading   **127**

Introduction

"Success could be defined as the continued expansion of happiness, and the progressive realisation of worthy goals. Success is the ability to fulfil your desires with effortless ease"

Deepak Chopra

Have you ever asked yourself the question: Is there more to life?

This question often gets asked when we go through a life-changing experience, such as illness, divorce, loss of job or death of a loved one. Or we may just reach middle-age and suddenly realise that we haven't done the things we always dreamed of doing.

There is more to life than we are led to believe. Life is not just about getting through your days and coping with what is thrown your way. It is a wonderful opportunity to create and grow and become more of who you are. It offers endless possibilities for joy, happiness, aliveness and fulfilment.

Somewhere along the way most of us stopped believing in our dreams. We stopped believing in our ability to create the life we really want. The magic disappeared and our life became mundane and routine.

We all have needs, desires and dreams. We all have ideas about how we would like our life to be. What is it that you want? What would you like to change? How would you like to feel? How would you like your life to be?

This book is about rediscovering your dreams and feelings of aliveness. It is about unlocking your potential, and bringing your unique talents into the world. It is about creating a successful and prosperous life — the life of your dreams.

You already possess the innate ability to create whatever it is you want. You have within you all the wisdom, knowledge, talents and creative power you need. A creative force lies within you right now; a well-spring of unlimited power just waiting for you to use it.

This book shows you how to harness that power. It contains the seven keys that will assist you in manifesting a wondrous, joyous and fulfilling life. With these seven keys you will be able to unlock your potential and unleash your creative power.

These are the seven keys to success and prosperity and consequently happiness. Living prosperously involves having the power to create the life you want. Living successfully involves having the skills and tools to bring your desires and dreams into reality. You are successful and prosperous to the degree that you are experiencing a life filled with joy, love and aliveness.

Success is not a destination — it is not that fleeting moment when you attain your goal; nor is it a place where you finally arrive. Success is a journey — it is the process of pursuing your dreams and goals; of self-discovery, becoming more, and expressing your unique talents in the world.

Prosperity does not refer only to money and material wealth. Lasting feelings of prosperity are dependent upon our internal experience. We feel prosperous to the degree that we regularly experience joy, happiness, aliveness, love, peace, balance and fulfilment.

May the *Seven Keys to Success, Prosperity and Happiness* assist you to rediscover your dreams; to harness and unleash your creative power; to become more of who you really are; to create the life you want and re-awaken the wonder, magic and mystery that is life.

Key No 1
DISCOVERING YOUR REAL NEEDS AND DESIRES

*"Desire ...is the nature of the soul, mind, heart and senses.
The soul is always willing to be more;
the mind is seeking to ... know more;
the heart is always longing to love more and have more;
and the senses are always wanting to enjoy more"*

John Gray

What are your real needs and desires?

What do you want in life? What do you want to be? What do you want to do? What do you want to experience? These are the questions you need to answer if you are going to experience authentic success, prosperity and happiness. Most of us don't know what we want, or alternatively our ideas of what we want are vague and fuzzy. If you want your creative power to work for you, then you must have a clear and specific direction. Vague and fuzzy goals do not have the energy to motivate you, nor to focus and direct your creative power.

The first step in creating a direction for yourself is to acknowledge those things you feel passionate about. What makes you feel alive? What inspires you? What excites you? What can you lose yourself in? What touches your heart?

Desire is a fundamental tool of your soul or Higher Self. It causes you to want to grow beyond your present existence. It creates within you a profound yearning for change that is irresistible. In this way your Higher Self encourages and facilitates your personal growth. Your Higher Self is always seeking to become more, and desire is its way of guiding you to uncover and express your unique talents.

Every one of us has unique talents related to a life purpose. Perhaps you are drawn toward children, teaching, politics, the environment, social issues, animals, gardening, agriculture, art, music, writing or healing. Finding your unique talents and expressing them in the world will make you feel alive and vital. Whatever your talents, they will involve making a positive contribution to others and the planet. When you combine the expression of your unique talent with service to humanity, you experience a truly successful and prosperous life.

If you are to know what it is you truly want, you will have to journey to the deepest part of your being and reflect on what makes you feel alive and passionate. Desire is a feeling within the soul, guiding you to your unique talents, self-expression and creativity.

Most of us are out of touch with this deepest part of our being. We are so caught up in the busyness of life — expending our energy on maintaining our comfort zones and ruts — that we neglect to reflect on what we truly want. We forget to stop and listen to the part of us that desires expression and creativity. We neglect to take notice of the subtle feelings, insights and messages we receive.

Begin your process of self-discovery by noticing what you feel passionate about; what excites you; what you feel drawn to. Allow quiet reflective time to acknowledge your feelings, desires, day-dreams and flashes of inspiration.

Finding your unique talents and path

Finding your unique talents and true path is a vital step to your experience of success and prosperity. Everyone of us has unique talents, a life purpose and a positive contribution to make to the world. Gary Zukav in Soul Stories calls this your "sacred task". When you are on your true path you are constantly becoming more of who you are — expanding, evolving and unlocking your potential.

Your authentic self-expression and true path can take many forms, and can change throughout your life. It involves creating the highest ideal of yourself throughout your journey. It is about honouring your Higher Self, listening to your inner voice and expressing it in a way that fosters depth, value, love and connectedness.

When you are expressing your unique talent, doing your "sacred task", contributing to the whole, you naturally experience joy, vitality, aliveness and fulfilment. Your life takes on added purpose and meaning. This is the path to which your desires, passion and flashes of inspiration are alluding.

Many of us are out of touch with these desires and subtle messages. However, your Higher Self is constantly sending you clues, signals, messages and guidance — you simply haven't always been open and receptive to receiving them. If you think back you might recognise the whisperings of your inner voice. There may have been times when you felt it stirring — perhaps yearning for something more, or a knowingness that there was something you must do.

Your deepest desires and dreams are the whisperings of your Higher Self. Your integrity also guides you to those things that are in harmony with the deepest part of your being.

Starting your process of exploration

If you do not know what you desire, or if your desires are still fuzzy and incomplete, start your process of self-discovery and exploration by getting a journal in which to write your insights, desires, reflections, ideas etc. It is invaluable to make notes about your inner journeys, for not only can reflection on your notes assist your personal and spiritual growth, but the process of writing itself often brings new insights. Here are some exercises to get you started:

Magic Wand

If you had a magic wand and were able to manifest the life of your dreams, what would you create for yourself? What would you like to experience? What have you always wanted to do some day? In what ways would you like to grow and evolve? Who would you love to become? What qualities would you love to possess? What would you love to contribute to others? What makes you feel vibrant and alive? What do you feel passionate about? What brings you great joy? What is important to you? Who would you share your experiences with? What qualities would your relationships possess? Allow yourself to use your imagination, to play and to feel.

What I Need

Write the following headings in your journal or notebook (one to a page).
- *Work/Service*
  (career; ambitions; contribution to society; finances etc)
- *Relationships*
  (love; home; partner; children; family; friends etc)
- *Mind, Body, Spirit*
  (personal growth; spiritual growth; physical well-being; exercise
- *Recreation*
  (sport; social; travel etc)

Sit quietly and reflect deeply on your spiritual, mental, emotional and physical needs in each of these areas. Write your thoughts down under each heading.

You may receive intuitive flashes and insights at a later time as you go about your everyday tasks — write these thoughts and feelings down under the corresponding heading, and build upon your self-knowledge.

What I No Longer Want

Write the following headings in your journal or notebook (one to a page).
- *Work/Service*
  (career; ambitions; contribution to society; finances etc)

- *Relationships*
  (love; home; partner; children; family; friends etc)
- *Mind, Body, Spirit*
  (personal growth; spiritual growth; physical well-being; exercise
- *recreation*
  (sport; social; travel etc)

Sit quietly and reflect upon what you don't want; what you would like to let go; what feels incomplete and lacking; and what you would like to change in each of these areas. Write your thoughts down under each heading.

Self-Discovery

Sit quietly and reflect on each of the following questions. Write your answers down in your journal.

- *What things do you love doing in your job?*
  (eg working with hands; organising; negotiating; helping others; challenges; working as a team; working alone; leading; communicating; information technology; working with machinery)
- *What are your interests or hobbies?*
  (eg sport; singing; dancing; art; self-improvement; cars; animals; machinery; gardening; the environment)
- *What sort of environment do you like working in?*
  (eg indoors; outdoors; with people; with machinery; with nature; with animals; physically active)
- *Are you drawn toward any particular area of work?*
  (eg healing; medicine; exercise; nutrition; politics; science; education; technology; environment; agriculture)

- *What issues do you feel strongly about?*
  (justice; equality; environmental; mental health; physical health; poverty; the homeless; the elderly; endangered species)
- *What are your strengths and talents?*

Rocking Chair

Imagine yourself at the end of your life, sitting in your rocking chair, reflecting back over your life. Write your answers to these questions in your journal.

- *What sort of life would you like to have had?*
- *What sort of things would you like to have experienced?*
- *Are there things you would like to have experienced more of?*
- *Are there things you would like to have experienced less of?*
- *What gave your life purpose and meaning?*
- *Reflect upon what you need to do differently now to live your ideal life.*

Understanding the essence of what you desire

The experience of authentic success and prosperity involves becoming aware of the essence behind your desires. To understand the essence ask yourself what feelings and experiences you associate with what you are desiring? It is always the feelings and experiences that you are seeking, not the object itself.

What deeper needs would be satisfied if you had your dream job, a loving relationship, a new car, more money? What are the feelings and experiences that you believe these things will bring — (security; freedom; social status; self-esteem; inner peace; aliveness; love; happiness; approval)? Do you seek them to make the loneliness or emptiness go away?

When you understand the feeling and experiences you are seeking, you find that there may be many other ways of fulfilling your needs. Acknowledging your authentic needs opens you up to seeing the many opportunities to fulfill your needs. Instead of being narrowly focussed on one thing, you open to the myriad of possibilities and can choose the path that serves your higher good.

Understanding the essence of what you desire, assists you to distinguish between the voice of your Higher Self and the false voice of ego.

The essence behind false desires can be a need to "fill the void" "stop the pain". This is co-dependence and produces an unhealthy need for a "quick-fix". This is the reason people become addicted to alcohol, tobacco, drugs, shopping, sex, gambling, eating, etc — their experience temporarily "fills the void" "stops the pain". There are however, more subtle forms of co-dependence, so ensure that your reasons for wanting something are not to chase empty, hollow, scared feelings away. Filling the void with quick-fix, feel-good things will never produce lasting feelings of fulfilment.

The essence behind false desires can be a need "to prove something to others" "get approval from others". This is a low self-esteem and self-worth issue. The desire may come from the need to prove that you are successful or worthwhile. Or it may come from the need to get someone's love and approval. Either way, achieving your desire will not produce lasting feelings of fulfilment.

Invest time in understanding what your authentic needs are. How will they change and expand your life? How will they assist you to become more of who you are?

Giving your desires and new ideas time to germinate

Whilst your desires and dreams are still seeds, it is beneficial to allow them time to germinate and develop strength before you share them with others. This is a time for your energy to be directed toward nurturing your dream. It is a time of building confidence and trust in yourself, your talents and inner guidance.

If you share your dream with others too soon, you put yourself in the position of having to explain, justify and rationalise your desire. You do not want your energy, focus or direction interrupted at this time. You do not want the flow of your creative thoughts to cease because your energy is now directed toward seeking approval. If you get a negative response from others too soon, it can cause you to return to your comfort zone and release your dream prematurely.

Likewise, don't stop the flow of your creativity by becoming impatient with yourself or the time you are taking. Allow your desires and ideas time to grow. Learn to treat your desires and ideas with the love and respect they deserve. Being impatient with the process or criticising yourself will stop your creative flow.

When your ideas and your self-confidence are somewhat developed, you may want to share your ideas with supportive friends who celebrate and encourage your self-expression.

Key No 2
CONNECTING WITH YOUR CREATIVE SOURCE

"Source means the supply of infinite love, wisdom and energy in the universe. For you, source may mean God, or the universal mind, or the oneness of all, or your true essence"

Shakti Gawain

Your Higher Self

When you are out of touch with your soul, your Higher Self, you lose your connection to the Creative Source and are cut off from your inner guidance and intuition. To some degree we are all out of touch with our Higher Self, intuition and instincts by virtue of the demands of modern Western society.

We have become overly identified with our intellect and "doing", at the the expense of our intuition, imagination and "being". We have learned to focus upon those things outside us and to experience them through five of our senses — sight, sound, taste, smell, touch. Being in touch with your Higher Self requires you to focus on what is happening inside you, and this can be greatly assisted and enhanced when you experience it through your sixth sense of intuition.

Our inner guidance and intuition is at the very core of us. When we neglect to nurture our spiritual nature, we become overly concerned with our logical, rational mind and caught up in the "busyness" of life. We become out of balance between thinking and feeling. Nurturing a relationship with your Higher Self is a gradual process, requiring you to spend quiet time alone. Quiet time in which to acknowledge and nurture your connection to the Creative Source. Quiet time to reflect on who you are;

what you want to become; what you value; and what are your authentic desires. When you take time to just be in the moment you tap into the Creative Source — the underlying energy of life from which all else flows.

Inner wisdom and guidance about your future path and direction often comes to you whilst you are in a quiet, reflective, peaceful state. Dreams, desires, new ideas, insights, feelings and flashes of inspiration come after you have tapped into this energy.

In our normal every-day state, our busy, noisy minds leave little room for inner wisdom or guidance to come through to us. In fact, the incessant chatter and thoughts that occupy most of our time are a drain on our creative energy, clarity and focus. When you quieten your mind and the noise ceases, you clear the way for creative energy, inner wisdom and guidance to flow freely.

A balance between "being and doing" must be effected if we are to be truly successful and prosperous. Being and doing compliment each other and enhance our experience of success and prosperity. Your quiet, reflective, "being" times are the source of dynamic ideas, rejuvenation and creative self-expression. Your "doing" times are for working out how to bring your ideas, creative self-expression and goals into reality.

If you do not create quiet time for yourself — time for meditation, reflection and being — then it is difficult to hear your inner guidance. Even if you have a knowing that you "desire something more" or that "something has to change", if you don't slow down to listen to the whisperings, you will not hear the message.

A period of meditation or reflection, a time of "being" is essential for connection to your Higher Self, from which flows inner wisdom and guidance. You cannot give expression to your creativity and unique talents, if you do not give them time or opportunity to reveal themselves. When you foster a relationship with your Higher Self, you access your potential — all that is you, all that is possible.

Connecting with your Creative Source involves making a regular practice of "being" in whatever way works for you. Meditation, visualisation and reflection are a wonderful way to connect with your Higher Self, as is quiet time spent in nature. However it does not necessarily require you to remain physically still — a state of being can be achieved whilst gardening, painting, sculpting, dancing, writing or walking — through any practice that you find relaxes you and quietens your busy thoughts.

Connecting with your Higher Self through meditation

Ensuring no interruptions, sit or lay in a comfortable position and close your eyes. Focus your attention inward, and begin to notice the rise and fall of your natural breath. Then begin taking deep, full breaths. Spend a few minutes breathing deeply and feeling yourself relax as you do so. As you breathe in imagine filling yourself with life-giving energy, and as you breathe out imagine all worries, negativities and concerns floating away. Allow yourself to experience feelings of beauty, gratitude and love.

Feel yourself connecting with your Higher Self — this is the experience of love, safety, and peace. Just allow yourself to "be" in this space and experience the tranquillity. Notice any thoughts or images that you may have, but don't engage in a conversation with them. Notice any outer noises or distractions — but just let them go. Enjoy your experience in the now moment.

Ideally, spend 20-30 minutes in a meditative state and then bring yourself gently back to waking consciousness — opening your eyes and stretching. Take a moment to reflect upon your inner experience and make notes in your journal.

Inner Guidance and Intuition

Your Higher Self communicates to you through intuition. There are many different forms of communication — words, images, symbols, bodily sensations, gut feelings or a sense of "knowing".

Opening to your intuition, and listening to your inner voice can be difficult because your ego-voice is so much louder. Whilst your inner voice is attempting to guide you to your true path with its subtle whisperings, your ego-voice is overriding it with loud, often fearful, thoughts. Learning to differentiate between the two can be difficult at first, but you will become skilled at it as you gain in self-awareness. One of the key ways to recognise your ego-voice is through the presence of fear — confusion, scepticism, anxiety, worry, negativity. Therefore when choosing a direction in life, follow the path that feels joyous — for love, clarity and peace are the feelings of your inner voice.

One of the ways your Higher Self communicates to you is through feelings. Feelings can often be felt in the body. The most common intuitive sensation is a feeling in the pit of your stomach that gives you a warning about the action you are about to take; or a knowing ("gut feeling") that you must take a certain action, even though it may appear to defy logic. Whenever you feel a heavy sensation or reluctance to continue, it is your Higher Self communicating to you that you are not following your true path, or that the action you are about to take is not in your best interest. When you feel light and joyful your Higher Self is guiding you to your true path.

When you follow your heart you find that doors open for you and life supports you. One of the ways life supports you is through synchronicity or coincidences. Synchronicity is the experience of being in the right place at the right time. You experience synchronicity when you think of someone just before they ring you; when opportunities appear and doors open at the right time; when you meet someone with the knowledge or information you need; overhear conversations that impart information you need; pick up a book with a message for you; receive a message from a movie or song. As we follow our true path we draw to ourselves the experiences we need, as we need them.

Your Higher Self also communicates to you through insights and flashes of inspiration. You may receive images or thoughts about your future direction or how to overcome obstacles. When faced with choices your intuition will guide you to the path of your greater good.

Your nightly dreams are also a great source of inner wisdom and guidance, and as with any inner work, quiet reflection is vital to interpreting their unique symbology and messages.

If you are to hear the subtle whisperings of your inner voice, you must make time for meditation, reflection and silence.

Asking Your Higher Self for Inner Guidance

In a meditative state, when our mind is quietened, we are able to get in touch with our inner wisdom — the source of knowing that lies within us. In this state of expanded awareness we are able to see with clarity.

- *Clarity In Your Question*

Select an issue, question or challenge for which you would like an answer. Be specific about the question you want an answer to.

- *Enter Into A Meditative State*

Ensuring no interruptions sit or lay in a comfortable position and close your eyes. Focus your attention inward, and begin to notice the rise and fall of your natural breath. Then begin taking deep, full breaths. Spend a few minutes breathing deeply and feeling yourself relax as you do so. As you breathe in imagine filling yourself with life-giving energy, and as you breathe out imagine all worries, negativities and concerns floating away. Feel yourself connecting with your Higher Self — experience the love, safety and tranquillity.

- *Ask Your Question*

Ask your question whilst in a meditative state and then let go. Remain open and receptive to receiving an answer, both in meditation and afterwards.

- *Bring yourself gently back to waking consciousness — opening your eyes and stretching. Take a moment to reflect on your inner experience, and make notes in your journal.*

Key No 3
HARNESSING AND UNLEASHING YOUR CREATIVE POWER

"I like to think of myself as an artist, and my life is my greatest work of art.
Every moment is a moment of creation, and each moment of creation contains infinite possibilities"

Shakti Gawain

The Process of Manifestation

Manifestation is the process whereby you bring your desires, ideas, dreams and goals into reality. It involves harnessing and directing your creative power. It involves working with the energy of your imagination. Everything in and around us is energy, and learning to work with energy is the basis of manifestation.

We are creating in every moment of our life — from simple creations such as cooking, decorating our home and nurturing our garden, to more complex self-expressions of our uniqueness — creations of art, inventions, writing. We also create collectively. Our collective energy co-creates such things as the quality of our human relationships — the degree of cooperation, equality and empathy we bring to them; the health or decay of our environment; and common thought-forms and beliefs about the nature of reality.

Thoughts

All of our thoughts are energy which have the potential to manifest. Everything ever created was first a thought in somebody's mind. Your creative power is the power of your imagination — your thoughts and images. Your imagination is your link to your Higher Self and your Creative Source. It has the ability to reach out to possibilities and the power to engage your emotions and motivate your actions. To unlock your potential you will need to learn to work with the creative power of your imagination.

You are always creating whether you are aware of it or not. You firstly create in your imagination through your thoughts, ideas and feelings. You attract to you whatever is most in your thoughts and feel most deeply about. If you want to enjoy more success and prosperity in your life, you must become aware of your thoughts. Do you regularly entertain thoughts of love or fear; abundance or scarcity; self-worth or unworthiness? What you radiate outward through your thinking is what you attract into your life. You are using this creative power all the time. If you are not directing it consciously to create the experiences you want, then you are using it unconsciously.

Your thoughts are like magnets, attracting energy, people and situations matching your expectations. If your thoughts are filled with unnecessary worry, fear and negativity — worrying about what may happen and fearing the worst — then you will attract these negative energies. On the other hand, if you are confident in your abilities and expect to experience joy, satisfaction and fulfilment, you will attract positive circumstances.

If you are to experience a successful and prosperous life, then you must harness this creative power and direct it. Your thoughts and images should be directed toward experiencing your desires, achieving your goals — and doing so with joy, love and faith. You create a more prosperous and successful life for yourself by learning to think in bigger and unlimited ways. What you consistently think and feel determines your beliefs.

Beliefs

Beliefs are the assumptions and expectations you hold about reality. If you have consistent thoughts, feelings and expectations about failing, you will form the belief you are a failure. If you have consistent thoughts, feelings and expectations about success, you will believe you are a success.

Many of us think our beliefs are true and cannot (and should not) be changed. But our beliefs are merely assumptions and expectations we hold about reality — created by thoughts and feelings. Every experience you have is created by your beliefs. You attract the people, events and circumstances mirrored in your belief system.

Your beliefs are powerful forces when creating your life. They can either support and encourage you, or limit and discourage you. Your beliefs are a reflection of your consistent thoughts, feelings and expectations.

Your core beliefs of yourself, the world and others were crystallised in childhood. You may believe life wasn't meant to be easy, or you may believe it is an exciting, challenging mystery.

You may believe you can't trust others because they are greedy and selfish, or you may believe others are generally loving and generous. You might believe life simply happens to you and you are at the mercy of luck, fate or God, or you may believe, you can create your own reality.

We all have beliefs about life, the world and ourselves, which in turn affect our relationships, health and our experience of success and prosperity. They influence the way we react to events. They produce patterns of thinking and behaviour that we will act out forever if we are not aware we can change them. These repeated patterns become our robotic way of reacting to situations, believing this is the way it is.

You have set in your mind the limits of your success and prosperity, based on beliefs. You will accomplish only that which you believe is possible.

Most of us are labouring under beliefs which limit our experience of success and prosperity, cause hardship and suffering, and limit our potential. Here are some common beliefs limiting our experiences:

- I don't have what it takes (internally) — strength, courage, confidence, motivation

- I don't have what it takes (externally) — money, time, luck, opportunities, I'm too old; too young; too shy; too stupid; too inexperienced; too set in my ways

- Successful and prosperous people were born that way — they have what it takes
- Nothing ever goes right for me
- It is too hard or overwhelming
- Other people always take advantage of me
- I don't deserve to be happy
- There are no opportunities — jobs are scarce; money is scarce
- Life is a struggle
- Life isn't fair
- The world is a dangerous, hostile place — you've got to watch your back
- Life is meaningless "life is a bitch and then you die"

A vital step in creating the life you want, is the awareness of being able to change your beliefs. You cannot harness and direct your creative power until you are aware your thoughts and beliefs are optional choices.

Choices

You can choose to nurture and expand thoughts and beliefs supporting you and empowering your experience of success and prosperity. You can also choose to change and release those thoughts and beliefs which disempower you and limit your experience of success and prosperity.

Although we have limitless possibilities of choice in every moment of our existence, we don't consciously use this power. We are making choices in every moment about every thought we have, every word we speak and every action we take, whether we are aware of it or not. However, most choices are made unconsciously based on our beliefs. We react automatically, without considering conscious choices.

When you bring choices to the level of your conscious awareness, you enable choice between creating anew or robotically reacting. If you continue to react to your programmed beliefs, attitudes and expectations then you will receive more of what has already been created.

Look at all the areas of your life. Where do you feel it is incomplete or lacking? Have you always been dissatisfied with these areas of your life? Are your thoughts, beliefs and expectations in these areas disempowering?

Choosing to change them, will create more opportunities — the choice is yours. Your choices create your experience and shape your life.

Taking responsibility for creating your experiences

Taking responsibility for creating your experiences involves awareness of your creative power and ability — your thoughts, beliefs, attitudes and expectations. It also involves being aware of your infinite choices in every moment. You contribute toward the creation of every situation in your life — good or bad — with the way you use your creative power.

Responsibility is generally a misunderstood concept. We often use the word to blame others — "they were responsible!". Or alternatively to blame ourselves — "I am responsible — it is all my fault". However, there is a difference between being responsible and blaming ourselves.

When you take responsibility for creating your experiences, you empower yourself. Realising you are responsible for your beliefs and attitudes naturally. You are responsible for the choices you make.

When you blame yourself or others for your experiences, you feel victimised. Likewise, you feel victimised if you believe you have to deal with what life throws at you. This is a disempowering attitude, assuming you have no choice. Blame prevents you from taking responsibility for your life and renders you powerless to create any changes.

Responsibility is an attitude toward life. An attitude acknowledging you have creative power, and you can choose how to direct this power. A vital step toward changing your future, is to take responsibility for where you are right now — putting it simply your thoughts and expectations have placed you in your current reality.

Life as a Mirror

The prosperity process involves acknowledging your reality is an external form of whatever you are imagining inwardly. Our external reality is a mirror, reflecting back to us our internal reality. Most people misunderstand this concept, confusing cause and effect. They think prosperity is an external issue and must therefore be dealt with externally (ie, I wish for lots of money, because then I'll be happy, excited, content and secure).

In fact, the reverse is true. First you must resolve the issue internally before expressing or manifesting the external "reality". It is our internal experience of success and prosperity that flows, over into our external world, not vice versa.

Whatever your experiences, whatever you have or don't have, whatever the quality of your relationships — they are the results of the choices you have made — choices based on your inner thoughts, images, and beliefs.

These inner thoughts, images and beliefs become subconscious patterns. That is, over time they become so ingrained, you respond to them without them entering your consciousness. It becomes your lifes pattern. However, if they are limiting your experience of success and prosperity, in order to change them you will need to identify and bring them to consciousness. It is only when you are consciously aware of your beliefs you can choose to change them.

Understand what you believe is true for you, regardless of whether your belief is accurate or not. Therefore, don't judge your beliefs by how accurate they are, but rather by how encouraging and supportive they are.

To hold onto a belief and behave in a way that is not supporting or guiding you toward your desired outcome, will only lead to more discouragement.

Take a careful look at areas of your life which you consider successful — what are your empowering beliefs in these areas? Take a careful look at areas which are painful, incomplete or lacking — what are your disempowering beliefs in these areas?

What does your outer life show you about your inner thoughts, images and beliefs?

Life As A Mirror

Begin your process of discovering your beliefs by looking at your life.

What does your external reality reflect back to you?

- *Choose an area of your life you are dissatisfied with and write about it in your journal.*

- *Step outside your emotions about this challenging area, viewing the situation as if it belonged to someone else.*

- *Ask what must this person believe about her/himself, others or life to have created this situation? As you write, notice those beliefs you resonate or react strongly to — for they will likely be your own limiting beliefs.*

- *Spend time in quiet reflection, and make notes concerning your insights in the journal.*

Finding Your Limiting Beliefs

This exercise helps you access your unconscious beliefs about yourself, life and others:

• Choose 2-5 things you want to change or have happen in your life, but have not as yet started moving toward, writing them in your journal.

• Look at the desires you have written and adjacent each of them write the reason/excuse as to why you haven't as yet accomplished it in your life, or even started moving toward it (eg I am not smart enough; I'm too old; too young; it costs too much money; I've made my bed and now I must lay in it; it's too hard; my mum/dad wouldn't approve; I don't have enough time; It would be selfish; I'm too scared).

• Notice if your reasons/excuses contain a common theme. These common themes will lead you to your limiting beliefs.

Attitude

Our experience of success and prosperity is not dependent upon what happens to us. Rather it is dependent upon how we react to what happens to us. Success and prosperity is ultimately an inner experience, flowing over into our outer life.

Although we can influence the direction of our life, there will no doubt be unexpected challenges along the way. We cannot control everything in life, nor would we want to — that would detract from the mystery, adventure and excitement of life. But we can choose how we will react to challenges.

It is your attitude toward life which determines your relationship to the outside world. Your attitude is swayed by your beliefs. The interpretation and meaning you assign to the challenges encountered, and the conclusions you draw are coloured by beliefs. In fact, nothing has any meaning in and of itself — meaning is open to your interpretation. Your thoughts, beliefs and expectations powerfully influence the interpretations you give to the events in your life. In turn, those interpretations determine your attitude.

People who experience success and prosperity choose to have an optimistic attitude, and to focus on what they can learn from challenging situations. Regardless of how impossible, challenging or negative something may seem. Choosing to think in terms of possibilities, they see challenges as stepping stones to greater success. They find a 'gift' or a learning experience within adversity.

Declaring Your Intentions

The function of declaring your intention is to attract to yourself that which you desire. It gives your Higher Self clear and precise instructions about what you want to create; who you want to be; what you want to experience. It also focuses and channels your energy — your thoughts and feelings — on what you want to experience.

Your intentions, born out of your desires, have energy behind them to attract to you that which will assist in bringing you closer to what you want to experience. Declaring your intentions allows your Higher Self and Creative Source to assist you — with insight, flashes or inspiration and synchronicity.

Create a List of Your Intentions

Create a list of your intentions and put them somewhere where you can read them daily — ideally somewhere you will see them first thing in the morning — your bedroom, bathroom etc. Here are some examples:

It is my intention to experience energy and creativity.

It is my intention to radiate compassion and understanding.

It is my intention to experience a successful and prosperous life.

It is my intention to attract opportunities to me.

It is my intention to become a Teacher/Naturopath/Dancer.

It is my intention to own my own home.

It is my intention to have an enriching, loving, equal relationship.

It is my intention to exercise and nourish myself appropriately.

It is my intention that my body regenerate itself and emanate health.

Creative Visualisation

Having declared your intentions, you can learn to use your natural creative imagination to support you in creating them. In the past your creative imagination may have hindered your experience of success and prosperity if you used it unconsciously to dwell on problems, failure and scarcity. When you worry about something or have negative thoughts about yourself, you visualise it in your mind. If you are experiencing problems, failure and difficulties in your life, it is because you first imagined it in your mind.

When you become aware that you create your reality through your thoughts, beliefs and mental imagery, you can choose to consciously create thoughts and images of health, abundance and well-being. Creative visualisation is the process whereby you mentally picture yourself achieving your goals and having your desires fulfilled.

Creative visualisations are more powerful when you bring strong emotions and feelings to them. Strong emotions determine the speed at which you manifest. Using your imagination to see yourself having your desires and achieving your goals — and generating strong emotions of joy, happiness, excitement, enthusiasm and optimism — is the essence of creative visualisation.

In addition to experiencing strong emotions during your visualisations, you can use all of your senses. Using your senses of sight, smell, taste, touch and hearing makes your image come alive and has a far greater impact on your subconscious.

Creative Visualisation

•State your Intention.
State to yourself what it is that you desire. Ensuring it isn't fuzzy and unclear (eg I want to be successful). If it is, you need to spend some time becoming clear about what it is you need to do to bring about the feeling of success? Achieving what sorts of things would make you feel successful?

•Connect with Your Creative Source.
Ensuring you won't be interrupted, sit or lay in a comfortable position and close your eyes. Focus your attention inward, and begin noticing the rise and fall of your breath. Then begin taking deep, full breaths. Spend a few minutes breathing deeply and feeling yourself relax as you do so. Breathing in imagine filling yourself with life-giving energy, and as you breathe out imagine all worries, negativities and concerns floating away. Feel your connection with your Higher Self.

•Use your Creative Power of Imagination
Visualise yourself doing whatever it takes to manifest your desire — having the courage to step out of your comfort zone; having the personal power required; moving through challenges and setbacks with ease; effectively planning and physically taking action; feeling adventurous, enthusiastic, motivated and fulfilled. See yourself achieving your desire with a positive attitude. See new doors opening because of your optimism. Experience yourself successfully journeying toward your goals, trusting your creative abilities and the

abundance of the universe. Allow yourself to experience your image and make it as real as possible.

•Expect that this or something better will come to you.

•Bring yourself gently back to waking consciousness — opening your eyes and stretching.

Affirmation

You can also harness your creative power through the use of affirmations. Affirmations are positive statements, declaring something already so — affirming that which you want to become; that which you want to achieve; or that which you want to manifest, as if it already exists.

We each have thousands of thoughts every day — thoughts, statements and ideas about ourselves, the world and other people. These thoughts, statements and ideas are the way we communicate with ourselves. These communications work hand in hand with our mental images to attract and create everything which is happening to us. We use our creative power of affirmation whether we are aware of it or not. Becoming aware of your self-talk requires awareness, dedication and commitment.

Affirmations should be repeated many times throughout the day. Any statement repeated over and over will impress itself upon your subconscious mind, where it will begin to manifest as your reality. You may choose to say your affirmations silently, out loud, or you may choose to write them down.

Affirmations should be stated in a positive way, giving a positive image to your subconscious mind. "I now enjoy my work" rather than "I no longer hate being at work".

They should also be stated as if they are already true — "I feel energetic" rather than "In the future I will feel energetic". Your subconscious mind takes what you say literally. If you wish for something in the future, it will give you what you wished for — something in the future, never arrives. It is for this reason it is important you state your affirmations as if they already exist.

Resistance to Affirmations

When you find yourself resisting your affirmations, do not be discouraged — this is natural. If you can travel to the centre of the resistance, you will find the core beliefs which are stopping you from achieving your desires.

Resistance can be experienced as negative thoughts; as fear; as pain in your body — such as in the pit of your stomach or throat; or as distractions — taking you away from your inner work.

Exploring Your Resistance

• *Choose an affirmation, and write it many times in your journal. Become absorbed in your affirmation, and allow yourself to feel any fears or pain associated with it.*

• *As you write your affirmation, notice the negative thoughts and make a note of them. It might go something like:*

I now have my own thriving business
You don't have what it takes

I now have my own thriving business
It's too scary and overwhelming

I now have my own thriving business
You're not courageous enough.

• *Reflect on the negative thoughts. It may be that your belief in your creative ability, or belief in your courage or intelligence need be strengthened in order to support your goal.*

• *In response to your negative thoughts, create affirmations which communicate confidence, supporting you in the creation of your desire.*

Examples being:

Negative Thought
You don't have what it takes.
Confident and Supportive Affirmation
With dedication I achieve everything I desire.

Negative Thought
It's too scary and overwhelming.
Confident and Supportive Affirmation
I have within me the strength to overcome all challenges.

Negative Thought
You're not courageous enough.
Confident and Supportive Affirmation
Courage is a natural part of my being.

Affirmations communicating confidence and supporting you in the creation of your desires

A powerful use of affirmations, is to communicate confidence to yourself, supporting you in the creation of your desires. For example, if it is your desire to become a teacher, and you find that the belief "I am not smart enough" is holding you back, you can support yourself by affirming "I am intelligent and achieve my dreams." Or if your desire/goal is to have a loving relationship, and you find the belief "I don't deserve to be loved" is sabotaging you, you can support yourself by affirming "I deserve to be loved. I now recognise my true worth".

Issue	Affirmation
Achieving	I can accomplish anything I choose.
	I have the power to live my dreams.
	I believe in my dreams and I believe in myself.
	With dedication I achieve all I desire.
Challenges	There is no challenge that I cannot conquer.
	I have within me the strength to overcome all challenges.
Change	I adapt easily to change.
	I move forward easily and effortlessly.
	I move beyond old limitations.
	It is comfortable for me to change.

Choice	My choices and possibilities are expanding every day.
Courage	Courage is a natural part of my being.
	I have the courage to face my fears and go beyond them.
Creativity	I am now creating my life as I want it.
	I am an open channel for creative energy.
	I honour and value my creativity and ideas.
Energy	I am filled with energy and enthusiasm.
	My energy is open and flowing in every area of my life.
Enthusiasm	I look forward with enthusiasm to the day ahead.
Expectations	My expectations are truly limitless.
Expression	I now express myself easily and effortlessly.
	It is safe for me to express myself.
	I communicate my needs .
Feelings	My feelings are normal and acceptable.
	I am now willing to experience all of my feelings.
	It is safe for me to feel.
Forgiveness	I forgive myself, others and all past experiences.
	I am forgiving and understanding with all people/myself.

Gratitude	I appreciate all that I am and all that I have.
Guilt	I grant myself forgiveness and move beyond the past.
Health	I experience only radiant health and energy.
Higher Self	I call upon my Higher Self to assist me in my understanding.
	My inner wisdom is guiding me now I acknowledge that I am linked with the unlimited abundance of the universe.
Integrity	I stand by my deepest truth and honour my self-expression.
Joy	I am alive to the joys of living.
Love	I feel love and compassion for all people, myself included.
Openness	I open myself to giving and receiving.
	I am open to life, love and joy.
Opportunities	I now attract opportunities to me.
	I now let miracles happen.
Patience	Through patience I achieve all I desire.
Peace	I am relaxed and peaceful.
Potential	I allow myself to be all I can be.
	I allow myself to have more than I ever dreamed possible.
	There is no limit to my potential.
	I am capable of everything I dream of doing.

Prosperity	I attract to myself all that I will ever need.
	Prosperity now comes to me easily and effortlessly.
	I accept prosperity and abundance into my life.
	I deserve to be prosperous and happy.
	I allow myself to be fulfilled.
Receiving	I am open to receiving my good.
	I remain open to receiving through unexpected channels.
Relationships	I now attract loving, enriching relationships.
Releasing	I now release the past with love.
	I let go easily, trusting that nothing leaves my life unless something better is coming.
Responsibility	I now take responsibility for my thoughts and actions.
	I take full responsibility for everything about me.
Self-Acceptance	I love and approve of myself.
	I am loving, lovable and loved.
	I acknowledge and honour every step I take.
	I love myself as I am.
	I am free to be me.
	I am a powerful, loving and creative being.
	I am a divine, magnificent expression of life.

Success	I am willing to be happy and successful.
	I am a success. I allow myself to feel successful.
Trust	I now trust the process of life.
	I am flexible and flow with the process of life.
	I choose to experience life as a delightful mystery.
	I trust my ever increasing ability to create abundance.
	I have complete faith and trust in the universe.
Worthiness	I now recognise my own true worth.
	I deserve the very best in life.
	I now allow myself to accept ...

Letting Go Of A Limiting Belief – Embracing A New Belief Visualisation

• *Choose a limiting belief*
Select a limiting belief you want to change, for example, "I don't have what it takes – I'm not courageous enough".

• *Make An Affirmation Which Encourages and Supports You.*
"Courage is a natural part of my being".

• *Enter Into A Meditative State*
Ensuring you won't be interrupted, sit or lay in a comfortable position and close your eyes. Focus your attention inward, and begin noticing the rise and fall of your natural breath. Then begin taking deep, full breaths. Spend a few minutes breathing deeply and feeling yourself relax as you do so. Breathing in, imagine filling yourself with life-giving energy. Breathing out imagine all worries, negativities and concerns floating away. Feel yourself connecting with your Higher Self – experience the love, safety and tranquillity.

• *Visualise Yourself Letting Go of Your Limiting Belief*
Imagine yourself entering into a brightly lit room – your room of beliefs. In the middle of the room there is a table, upon which lies a leather-bound book. Embossed on the book's cover in gold lettering is "My Beliefs and Attitudes". Open this book and on the first page see your limiting belief written "I am not courageous enough". With a feeling of love, joy and freedom, tear this page from your book. See yourself set fire to

the page and watch as it burns. Affirm that you release this belief with love. Turn back to your book of beliefs and attitudes and on a new page write your new belief — "Courage is a natural part of my being" See yourself writing each letter — do it in beautiful writing (perhaps calligraphy). When you are finished writing, look at your new belief and repeat it. Then close your book of beliefs.

• Bring yourself gently back to waking consciousness — opening your eyes and stretching.

• Support your new belief by affirming it to yourself frequently; write it down and put it where you can see it often.

Making A Wheel of Fortune

A Wheel of Fortune or Treasure Map is a visual blueprint of your desires and intentions. It is a blueprint of the way you want your life to be. You can be as creative as you wish when making it — cutting out pictures and powerful words from magazines, using affirmations, photographs, drawing, painting or symbols to represent your desires/goals. In my workshops I like to use a Wheel of Fortune — a circle divided into the four main areas of life. Thinking about your desires in all areas of your life ensures you are not neglecting or overdeveloping any area. It ensures you are leading a balanced lifestyle.

Your Wheel of Fortune is a visual reminder of what is important to you — what you want to experience in life. Hang it conveniently where you see it often. You can energise your desires/goals by experiencing strong feelings — joy, enthusiasm, happiness, fulfilment, excitement, love — whilst looking at it. One of my workshop participants has made this practice even more powerful by taking a photograph of her Wheel of Fortune which she can carry with her and look at often.

Allowing Change

When we attempt to force change, rather than allow gradual growth, we act against our essential nature.

Using our willpower to force behaviour, when our inner images are still ones of fear, doubt or insecurity will not work. If our internal images and willpower are at odds and are engaged in battle, our internal images will always win.

Allowing change involves patience and dedication. The "quick-fix" solution which your ego craves does not exist. Have your willpower support you, patiently and with dedication whilst you are changing your internal images.

Forcing change is not the right use of willpower. It will not bring about the ultimate change you desire. The correct use of willpower is to support and encourage you in patience, and dedication.

Key No 4
OVERCOMING OBSTACLES

*"Rather than pray for a life which is problem-free
ask for one which is solution-full.
Instead of requesting that God
remove the mountain before you,
seek the strength to climb it".*

Douglas Bloch

Gradual Journey of Discovery and Change

Your powerful beliefs about success and prosperity are operating at an unconscious level. Although you may no longer be conscious of them, they determine your feelings and reactions to every situation. If you are to experience a successful and prosperous life, you must discover and release those beliefs which stand in your way of seeing yourself as a creator of plenty.

This is a gradual journey of discovery and change. Whenever making any sort of change you are forced out of your comfort zone.

Comfort Zone

Whenever doing something out of the ordinary or making some sort of change, it may fall outside your comfort zone. We are all, to a degree resistant to change. — It is our way of trying to protect ourselves — it is our survival mechanism. When the feelings you experience are uncomfortable, you naturally become discouraged and return to familiar and comfortable thoughts, feelings and actions. Interestingly though, quite often the familiar patterns are not "comfortable"at all. In fact, thoughts, feelings and actions we label "uncomfortable" would bring about the most growth, aliveness, joy, happiness, love and fulfilment.

The uncomfortable feelings experienced in response to change can be labelled. "fear" Remaining in your comfort zone requires a lot of energy — energy expended avoiding thoughts, situations and experiences which might produce "fear".

Fear

We can feel fear simply contemplating taking a new action. In your imagination you create worst-case scenarios; relive past painful memories; and project future failures and humiliation. For the most part however, what you fear is not real, yet you react to the pictures of your imagination as if they were — such is the power of the imagination.

Fear is one of the major reasons we often do not allow ourselves to feel our authentic desires. Whenever you risk following your heart your imagined thoughts of failure or rejection are greater. If your self-expression is criticised or rejected, it hurts much more deeply. When you take risks you feel open, exposed and vulnerable and your fear of being hurt, rejected, criticised or failing is far greater. If you react to these negative thoughts and feelings, you will return to your comfort zone.

There is a common misconception we are not ready to take new action if we are experiencing feelings of fear or anxiety. If you believe this then you are never going to risk doing anything close to your heart. You are never going to stretch and grow. You will either put off your desire indefinitely; find excuses as to why it was a bad idea in the first place; or resist feeling your desires and block listening to your inner wisdom. This common belief assures that you will feel discouraged and guarantees inaction.

Understand we all feel some level of fear or anxiety when we make a decision to grow, change or do something new — fear of the unknown, fear of failure, fear of rejection, fear of being judged by others. All progress in life involves moving through the fear. If you allow yourself to feel the fear — to journey to its centre — you will find that its power over you immediately disappears.

Instead of resisting your fears, see every fear as representing an area of your potential that you have not yet developed; an opportunity to become more expansive. Unlocking and releasing your fears opens up your greater potential and can bring with it new insights and visions about who you can be.

Discovering and letting go of limiting beliefs and patterns can bring up enormous fear and resistance to change. The reason for this is because many of our beliefs were originally developed to protect ourselves — they are survival mechanisms developed in childhood. So even though our beliefs and patterns may be producing unpleasant life experiences, we hang onto them as they feel safe and secure. However, chances are that the beliefs which served you as a child, no longer serve you. Do they assist and support you in creating the life you want?

If you continue reacting to your fears, if you do not expand your comfort zone you will sabotage your creativity; your expression; your uniqueness; your fulfilment; your dreams; your growth; and your experience of success and prosperity. If you are to live a successful and prosperous life, you must accept a certain amount of fear and anxiety as a necessary part of the journey. Remember all progress in life involves moving through the fear. As we continue to grow, evolve and take new risks, we are going to experience fear. Have compassion for that part of you that is growing; for that area of your potential not yet developed.

When you change your beliefs and attitudes about fear, your experience of it transforms into something quite different. Instead of feeling paralysed by fear you begin to feel exhilarated, excited and motivated by it.

Journey To The Centre of Your Fear

This exercise can help acknowledge your fears. Your fears lose their power when you journey to their centre.

• *Enter Into A Relaxed State*
Ensure you won't be interrupted and sit or lay in a comfortable position and close your eyes. Focusing your attention inward, begin to notice the rise and fall of your natural breath. Then begin taking deep, full breaths. Spend a few minutes breathing deeply and feeling yourself relax as you do so. As you breathe in imagine filling yourself with life-giving energy, and as you breathe out imagine all worries, negativities and concerns floating away. Feel yourself connecting with your Higher Self – experience the love, safety and tranquillity.

• *Talk With Your Fear*
Visualise the part of you that is afraid – give it form. Perhaps you could see it as a small, frightened child. Encourage your fear to talk with you. Thank it for protecting you. Convey appreciation for it wanting to keep you safe. Discuss with it what you now want to experience. Explain how its current method of protection is actually hindering your experience of success and prosperity. Show it how it could better support you. Explore how you can both move in the same direction.

• *Return to Waking Consciousness*
Bring yourself gently back to waking consciousness – open your eyes and stretch. Whilst still in a meditative state, reflect upon your inner experience and make notes in your journal.

You Are Not Your Fears

Whenever fearful thoughts arise, observe them, allow yourself to feel them, but recognise that you are not them. Change your thoughts and beliefs from "I am fearful/anxious" to "The feeling of fear/anxiety is now passing through me". This allows you to feel your fear, but to also let it go. Remind yourself that it is not who you are — it is just an emotion you are experiencing.

Changing Your Attitude About Your Comfort Zone

Whenever you fall into the trap of believing it is more satisfying to stay in your comfort zone than to grow, change or take risks, do the following exercise. Your "comfort zone" will look very uncomfortable afterwards, and your desire/goal more enticing.

- In your journal write down one desire/goal that you have been putting off, because you would rather stay in your comfort zone.

- Write in a paragraph what it will cost you if you don't start moving toward your desire/goal. How will you feel? What will you miss out on? How will it affect your self-confidence now and in the future? How will it detract from your experience of success and prosperity? Allow yourself to feel this strongly.

- Write in a paragraph the benefits of taking action toward your desire/goal. How will it enhance your life? How will it affect your self-confidence now and in the future? How will you feel? Will you experience greater joy, freedom, aliveness? How will it add to your experience of success and prosperity? Allow yourself to feel this strongly.

Feeling and expressing all your emotions

Whether it be fear or another "negative" emotion, resisting it will not make it go away. In fact, when you resist something you continue to create it. Positive thinking is not about glossing over or suppressing your "negative" emotions. It is not about pretending that life's challenges don't exist. It is about having a positive attitude toward "negative" emotions. It is about having a positive attitude to life's challenges. The two are quite different.

Resisting our feelings and emotions, not only ensures we will attract more of what we are trying to resist into our life, it costs us a lot of energy. Energy which is focussed on suppressing our feelings and emotions, instead of making our dreams come true. This suppression of emotional energy causes you to become a semi-conscious being — reacting to life, rather than creating the life you want. It contributes to your lack of personal power. Suppression, numbing out and repression blocks your potential. When your energy is freed up, it can be re-channelled into creating the life you want.

Instead of resisting or suppressing emotions, journey to their centre. Allow yourself to feel them, and find constructive ways to express and release them. One very effective way of expressing your emotions is to freely write about them on paper, and then burn the paper as a symbol of your letting go. If you are angry at someone, write a letter telling them how you feel(felt), what you need(ed), and then release the pain by burning the letter. As your letter is burning it may be of assistance to repeat the affirmation "I bless you with love and release you from my life".

What emotions do you habitually suppress?

Emotions I Do Not Express

Look at the following list and reflect upon which feelings/emotions you habitually suppress or deny. What are your beliefs about the emotions you have difficulty expressing? What is the consequence of suppressing them (do they erupt in an explosion at a later date; do they cause illness; do they cause depression and lack of vitality?)

compassion	*anger*	*happiness*
love	*frustration*	*passion*
trust	*disappointment*	*excitement*
faith	*grief*	*sadness*
joy	*jealousy*	*fear*
peace	*hurt*	*vulnerable*
gratitude	*embarrassment*	*assertiveness*
enthusiasm	*fear*	*power*
tolerance	*guilt*	*vulnerability*

Feelings and emotions are not good or bad in themselves. They only become destructive when we suppress or deny them. When you travel to the centre of an emotion and fully experience it, the energy behind it transforms.

Whilst some people suppress their emotions, others feel them, but are unable to let them go. The intention behind feeling and expressing your "negative" emotions, should be to release them. Hanging onto past pain and reliving it over and over only attracts more of the same to you, and drains your creative energy.

Forgiveness

Forgiveness is a form of releasing and letting go of the past. Often we hold onto our anger and resentment to punish the other person, but in fact we only harm ourselves. A common misconception, is that to forgive is to condone the other person's actions, or to make the situation OK. But this is not forgiveness. You do not have to approve of the situation or condone the other person's behaviour in order to forgive. Nor do you have to pretend you were not hurt.

Forgiveness is an act of love and respect for yourself. Forgiveness means that you refuse to harbour anger, venom or hatred. It means letting go of blaming others for your circumstances, because not letting go would render you powerless — a victim. Forgiveness is an act of taking responsibility for your life — choosing what you hang onto and what you let go of.

Forgiveness is the most powerful thing you can do to release anger, resentment and critical judgment. It is also the most powerful thing you can do to release guilt and shame — forgive yourself. Forgiveness is a process of healing.

Creating Balance and Feeling of Wholeness

In modern Western society, we are inclined to view certain aspects of ourselves as acceptable and other aspects as not so. The consequence is becoming identified with only a tiny percentage of who we are — those qualities and aspects we label "acceptable". Any of the "unacceptable" parts are suppressed, repressed and buried. An important key to creating success and prosperity is exploring, balancing and integrating your disowned aspects. To feel whole and to live from a place of wholeness, you need to be in touch with all aspects of self.

The qualities and aspects which are denied do not leave you. Instead, they collect in the dark corners of our psyche like a shadow. The cause of the shadow is the division of everything in our lives into opposites — into "good" and "bad". Whilst we express those qualities and aspects of self we label "good", we cut ourselves off from those we consider not so. When you identify exclusively with one side of the duality, and repress the other, you begin to have a false view of reality and cannot move towards wholeness. When you become too one-sided you cut yourself off from your vital energy and creative impulses. Thomas Moore refers to this as "suppression of the life force".

Those qualities and aspects we have repressed, are actually valuable strengths — part of the greater whole. When you choose to live from a one-sided perspective, you disempower yourself. It becomes difficult to broaden your vision and to see other options. The more qualities and aspects of yourself that you discover and learn to express, the more wholeness you experience, and the more successful and contented you feel.

Exploring, balancing and integrating your disowned aspects involves recognising that opposites are not irreconcilable — opposing forces are only different aspects of the same thing. Both sides must be equally accepted and appreciated.

Masculine and Feminine

Each of us has masculine and feminine qualities contained within. Reliance on one aspect to the exclusion of the other will limit our experience of success and prosperity.

In modern Western society we have become overly identified with our intellectual, linear, logical, masculine qualities at the expense of our open, holistic, intuitive, imaginative, vulnerable, creative feminine qualities.

When we are overly identified with the masculine principle we experience separateness and alienation from ourselves, others and nature. New insights, deep feelings and dynamic ideas are prevented from entering consciousness. We may accomplish a great deal, but it lacks depth, value and meaning.

When we are overly identified with the feminine principle we experience oneness but have a reduced sense of self, independence, and our ability to control or act upon our insights and creative ideas is reduced.

Neither principle can realise its potential without merging with the other. Giving equal time and value to both the masculine and feminine energies within you, will ensure you attract, create and manifest your authentic desires — authentic desires which encompass value and meaning to all.

Giving and Receiving

Giving and receiving are another example of opposite energies and both need expression if you are to experience fulfilment and plenty in your world. Most of us are overly identified with the masculine principle — giving, and have difficulty with the feminine principle — receiving. However, giving and receiving are different aspects of the same thing — the flow of energy in the universe. To deny one is to deny the other.

Because giving and receiving are inextricably linked to our experience of success and prosperity, it is necessary to learn to value both energies. Many opportunities occur daily for you to balance these two energies. Learn to receive with gratitude — compliments, acknowledgments, appreciation, love. Learn to give to others freely. You don't have to give material objects — give love, appreciation, a smile, a silent blessing; give of yourself, your laughter, your authentic feelings. Make a decision to give to all those you come in contact with.

Learning to give and receive freely will create freely flowing energy in all areas of your life, enhancing your experience of success and prosperity.

Your Relationship with Money

Giving and receiving are inextricably linked to our relationship with money. Money represents the energy that flows out from us to the world (giving) and the energy that flows back to us (receiving).

Our financial circumstances reflect back to us our thoughts, beliefs and attitudes about money and/or the qualities it represents to us. Gaining a better understanding of what money represents to you will assist you in finding and changing any limiting thoughts, beliefs and attitudes you may have in relation to it.

What Does Money Represent To You

•*Sit quietly, reflect upon what money represents to you, and make notes in your journal. What deeper needs are satisfied by money? What are the feelings and experiences these things will bring you — power, success, recognition, security, freedom, happiness?*

•*Now explore your thoughts and feelings about the deeper needs that money would satisfy. If you feel that money will bring you success for example ask yourself the following questions (substitute (success) with the quality you identify with):*

If I were *successful* I would ...

If I were *successful* I wouldn't ...

My family think *successful* people ...

I think *successful* people ...

I think being *successful* would create the following pressures ...

I am not as *successful* as I'd like to be because ...

I see myself as *successful* when ...

I see myself as *unsuccessful* when ...

If I were *successful* other people might think ...

- *Can you see any patterns or limiting beliefs contained in your answers?*
Your limiting beliefs may be about:

Yourself	*I don't have what it takes to be "successful"*
Others	*"They will criticise/envy me if I'm successful"*
	"Successful people don't have any values"
The World	*"There are no opportunities out there, so why bother".*

- *Begin to change your patterns/limiting beliefs by choosing to think and act differently. Choose a new empowering belief and support it with visualisation and affirmations.*

Belief in Scarcity

There is a collective belief in scarcity — that there is not enough to go around for everyone. We believe there is insufficient — food, land, opportunity, love, money. This collective belief creates power struggles and competition. When you believe in scarcity, you necessarily believe your success must be at the expense of another, or if someone else succeeds you will miss out. Obviously from this perspective, it is difficult to celebrate others successes and difficult to feel good about your own.

There is however no real lack or scarcity. The universe is a place of great abundance and there is more than enough to go around. The media would have us believe that we are experiencing an energy crisis — but all that exists in the universe is "energy".

We may be experiencing a challenge to change and use sources of renewable energy — such as wind and water — but there is no lack or shortage of "energy".

When you believe in scarcity, you envy other people's success and prosperity. To begin to change your belief from one of scarcity to plenty, celebrate other people's success and prosperity and see it as evidence of plenty. See too your own success and prosperity as adding to others prosperity. When you spend money, do so from a sense of adding to others prosperity. See money as a means for exchanging good for all. Our experience of plenty is only limited by our beliefs.

An off-shoot of this belief is feeling guilty about having too much whilst others live in poverty. However, remaining stuck in guilt and not taking responsibility for your own life is not going to help those living in poverty. When you change your belief in scarcity — to a belief in the abundance of the universe — you can then reach out to others in love and trust and assist them to discover their own power.

Self Sabotage

We each have impulses urging us to evolve and become more. At the same time we can have an equal urge of restraint. This inner war can result in self sabotage — taking actions inconsistent with your dreams and values. If you experience external success before your internal self-image is ready for it, it is likely you will sabotage your success. Don't allow yourself to become discouraged — as you change your internal self-image, thoughts and beliefs, your outer reality will reflect your true self.

Self-sabotage can also be a protection mechanism. If your past experiences have led you to the belief that success will lead to pain (eg when you have been successful others have criticised or judged you; or independent action led to punishment and pain in childhood) — then you may sabotage yourself. If every time you take a step toward your goal, you equate it with inevitable pain, this is hardly surprising. Once again, do not become discouraged — when you believe that success leads to happiness and fulfilment rather than pain, your self-sabotaging behaviour will cease.

Key No 5
FOSTERING AN ATTITUDE OF SUCCESS AND PROSPERITY

"Gratitude is one of the greatest secrets of a fulfilled life – it is cooperating with the Universe".

Rev Nancy Norman

Honouring your Worthiness to Receive

Feeling worthy is essential to being able to attract to yourself what it is you desire. If you feel undeserving, then you either will not attract opportunities to yourself or you will refuse to acknowledge those which appear.

If you find you are denying yourself good in any way, it is out of a lack of self-worth. Lack of self-worth is a result of not loving and accepting yourself as you are. It is a challenge that we all face to one degree or another.

Building the foundation of self-worth — love and acceptance of self — is the key to honouring our worthiness to receive. This process begins with not hiding behind a role or an image. If your self-worth is externally based and is dependent upon your image, your youth, your job, your social status or others' approval, then its foundation is shaky. External things are constantly changing, as will be your self-worth, if it is based upon them.

Internally based self-worth is constant — it does not depend on external circumstances. Authentic self-worth comes when you connect with your spiritual self and recognise that you are part of the infinite energy of love and wisdom, whatever that be for you. Loving yourself does not mean loving only your "good" points, it involves accepting yourself unconditionally as you are — regardless of your past experiences, current situation, strengths or weaknesses, successes or failures.

Creating self-worth involves listening to your inner wisdom, true feelings, authentic desires and acting upon them. It involves being true to yourself and respecting your inner flow — there is a time for "being" (rest, relaxation and rejuvenation) and "doing" (planning and taking action). It involves never criticising yourself for who you are or where you are.

Celebrate and enjoy all that you are and all that you have created. To reject any part of it is to reject a part of yourself. When you constantly criticise yourself you start to believe you have no value. Instead of focussing on what you do "wrong" and criticising yourself for it, focus on your abilities, talents and successes. Encouragement and statements of confidence in your ability are important boosters of self-worth.

Send messages to your subconscious that you are worthy by honouring yourself and doing things that nurture your soul — spend time in nature, listen to music, take time to, meditate, laugh, watch children playing, play an imaginative game with your children, do something artistic and creative, play. Allow some magic into your life.

Feeling worthy to receive is essential to being able to attract to yourself what you desire. Begin to build the foundation of self-worth by loving and approving of yourself.

Foundation of Self-Worth

Self-Acceptance
Love and accept all parts of yourself — mind, body and spirit.
Allow yourself to experience all your emotions, and find ways to express them constructively.
Treat yourself with compassion and understanding.

Self-Respect
Foster a relationship with your Higher Self.
Acknowledge your true feelings and desires.
Acknowledge your needs, desires, dreams and values.
Express yourself and live by your own truths.
Speak and act from a level of integrity and honesty that reflects your Higher Self.

Self-Responsibility
Take responsibility for your thoughts and beliefs.
Take responsibility for your choices.
Let go of guilt and feelings of unworthiness.
Let go of blame and feelings of victimisation.
Encourage yourself with statements of confidence in your ability.

Self-Assertiveness	*Be willing to take risks.* *Pursue your dreams, desires and goals with courage.* *Use your unique talents to serve humanity.* *Dare to follow the road less travelled.*

Gratitude

Gratitude helps dispel the belief in scarcity — there is not enough. When your heart is filled with gratitude, you focus on many blessings — on what you do have, rather than what you don't have. When you take the time to be grateful for the many things you are and have, your focus expands and opens your flow to greater prosperity. Gratitude is a magnetic energy, drawing to you more of the things you desire. Taking time to acknowledge the beauty, wonder, mystery, love and riches that surround you cultivates gratitude. Fostering feelings of thankfulness leads to ever-deepening levels of gratitude — gratitude for life's paradoxes and complexity. It goes beyond being grateful for obvious blessings and expands your vision and you also begin to see the gifts in challenging circumstances. You begin to see the gifts in adversity — the growth, strength, courage, compassion, change of attitude which has come about as a result of an assortment of experience. Practising gratitude in the face of adversity requires you to expand your vision to encompass a bigger picture.

At its deepest levels, gratitude consciousness acknowledges your connection to the Creative Source — the source from which all else flows. It aligns you with the harmony of this Universal Intelligence — knowing that there is a bigger picture, and trusting that all situations contain spiritual gifts.

Living in the Present Moment

Expressing gratitude for the miracles, wonder and beauty in your world requires you to be in the present moment. Being present in the moment involves letting go of worries about the future and releasing the pain of the past.

Louise Hay, reminds us that "the point of power is always in the present moment" Whatever you are choosing to think and believe in the now moment is creating your future. You are attracting your future through the quality of thoughts that you have this moment. You are creating yourself anew in this moment. All choices are made in the present moment.

Tips For Fostering Gratitude Consciousness

•Upon waking in the morning give thanks for the experiences you will have that day; and before going to sleep at night, give thanks for the experiences of your day — even the "bad" ones. They may serve to show you things about yourself which need healing; they may strengthen you; they may make you a more compassionate person; they may be the catalyst for your searching and awakening. Practice seeing the hidden gift in so-called "negative" experiences.

•When you find yourself worrying about the future, or feeling the pain of the past — focussing on what is lacking or wrong — change your focus and be grateful for all your blessings.

•Throughout the day say the words "thank you" to yourself and others. Speak words of gratitude, success, abundance and prosperity instead of words of lack, failure, fear and scarcity.

•Spend time in quiet reflection and/or meditation, appreciating the Wonder and mystery of life, and the wonder and mystery of your own magnificent expression.

•Spend time in nature, experiencing the now moment, and appreciating nature's beauty and wonder.

•Keep a gratitude journal and write on a daily basis 10+ things you are grateful for. You will start to be grateful for such things as the smile of a stranger, the laughter of children, a beautiful rainbow, a touching song.

- *Don't take things for granted — this drains you of the joy you could be experiencing.*

- *When we live with grateful hearts we feel full and complete and quite magically we draw to us the things we desire.*

Release

You must release that which you no longer need in order to make room for the new. This applies on the spiritual, mental and physical planes of life. Clutter in your life leads to more clutter. When you hold onto the outgrown and worn out, you usually do so from fear of loss. This fear will always cut off the possibility of more. In fact, fear of any kind keeps you bound to something.

Letting go of that which no longer serves you, forms a vacuum into which your good can flow. Letting go actually opens the way for new channels of supply. Take a look at your life and decide which ideas, relationships, beliefs and situations no longer work for you. Symbolically declare your intention to release the old to the Universe by cleaning out the clutter in your home. Release old ways of being and open the way for new opportunities.

Releasing is always done with an attitude of love and gratitude. Attempting to get rid of something because you fear it or hate it is not the same thing as releasing. In fact your intense emotions of fear and hate will actually bind you to the very thing you are trying to get rid of. You cannot release something you fear or something you hate. Therefore you must first be grateful for it — see how it has served you and benefited you. In order to change a situation, you must first accept it the way it is. In order to move forward, you must first make peace with where you are.

Listed below are some common limiting patterns needing to be released if you are to experience a successful and prosperous life. Can you see any of your own patterns? Begin to create space for the new by releasing these patterns with love and compassion.

Need for Perfection
Pre-occupation with being and doing things the one right way; your focus is upon what is missing and you judge yourself and others harshly.

I now release my fear of being criticised.
I now affirm that the best I can do is good enough.

Need for Approval
Pre-occupation with getting the approval of significant others; your focus is upon what others think and you adjust your life in order to get other's approval; you find it hard to know what your authentic feelings and desires are.

I now release the fear that I am unloved.
I now affirm that I am lovable for who I am.

Need for Admiration
Pre-occupation with achievements and self-importance; you seek to feel special through admiration of your successes, career or social status; you feel you are loved for what you are, not who you are.

I now release the fear of failing and being humiliated.
I now affirm that I have value regardless of my achievements.

Need to be Special	Pre-occupation with being so special (evolved, sensitive, creative) that no one can understand you; you seek to avoid seeing yourself as ordinary; you constantly search for Self and authenticity; can feel so different that to cope you escape by withdrawing and feeling hopeless.

I now release the fear that I am unimportant.
I now affirm that I am bringing something good and valuable into the world.

Need to be Intelligent	Pre-occupation with logic, reason, ideas and facts; you detach from your feelings and from others; you avoid sharing or any real intimacy; you withdraw from life and become a spectator; becoming stuck in thinking and avoid taking action.

I now release my fear of being violated by others.
I now affirm that I have faith in others and the future.

Need for Security	Pre-occupation with feeling safe and secure; you seek to avoid anything that brings up feelings of anxiety and fear;

your focus is upon perceived danger or attack; you avoid making decisions and taking risks.

I now release my fear of being abandoned and alone.
I now affirm that I meet challenges with confidence.

Need For "Speed"   Pre-occupation with excitement, enthusiasm, excess and fun; you seek to avoid anything mundane or "negative" consequently you are impatient with any process, do not go into anything in depth, and have difficulty with commitment.

I now release my fear of being deprived.
I now affirm that I find satisfaction in ordinary things.

Need to Control   Pre-occupation with things going exactly as you want them to; you seek to feel strong and avoid any signs of weakness; you feel as if others will take advantage of you and lack trust in a friendly universe.

I now release my fear of vulnerability and intimacy.
I now affirm that I can be gentle without being afraid.

Need to avoid Conflict   Pre-occupation with everything going smoothly; your focus of attention is upon avoiding conflict and consequently you take the path of least resistance; you deny your own feelings, by merging with other's points of view to avoid conflict.

I now release my fear of separation.
I now affirm that I actively embrace all life brings.

Key No 6
SETTING GOALS AND TAKING ACTION

*"True success is not just attaining goals,
it is attaining goals which are worth attaining".*

Tom Morris

Goals

Goals give your creative energy a clear focus and direction. When you have identified your authentic desires, you can then begin setting goals. A goal is quite different to a desire. Goals give your desires direction. Goals give you a clear vision of where you want to go and are a commitment to focus your energy in a particular direction.

Without a clear vision your creative energy has no direction. Further, when reflecting on how to bring your desire into reality, you become aware of all the possible roads you may take, and are able to choose the best routing.

Having clear goals does not mean you are fixed to those goals. Rather they are a focus and direction for your creative energy. If, along the way, you find a better way of achieving your desire, or discover new opportunities, then by all means review your options and adjust your goals accordingly.

Do not let thoughts of there being only one "right" way, or doubts about whether it would be better to pursue this or that stop you from setting meaningful goals. In fact, discovering what you want in life is facilitated by the process of setting goals. As you channel your creative energy into meaningful goals, new opportunities, new information and new ideas will present themselves to you. You learn by doing.

Goal Setting

When setting goals it is important to extend yourself, but not make your goals unrealistic. It is wonderful to have big dreams, but it is important to break your dream down into achievable parts — stepping stones to a bigger result. Comparing today with where you want to be causes unhealthy levels of stress and anxiety, therefore you need to break your dream down into stepping-stones. You need to plan on how to get from here to there.

Your short-term goals might include developing talents, replacing negative beliefs with positives, building self-worth, saving money, further studies or reading. Breaking long-term goals down into short-term is an important part of your success.

In his book Emotional Intelligence, Daniel Goleman refers to the state of "flow" in which we are motivated to become better and better at something. It is a state in which we become positive, energised and aligned with the task at hand, enabling outstanding performance. This motivated state only occurs in the zone between boredom and anxiety. If you don't extend yourself you become bored, and if you extend yourself too much you become anxious. Finding a balance between the two is essential to your state of flow. You can find this balance when you break your long-term into short-term goals down into short-term goals — stepping-stones to your greater success. Also important to your experience of success and prosperity is having all areas of your life working. One area in which you are not happy will affect every other aspect of your life. Make sure you keep every area of your life alive and balanced.

Goal Setting

Write these four headings one to a page in your journal (you can further divide these lists, if you want to explore some areas in more depth):

• *Work/Service (career; ambitions; contribution to society; finances etc).*

• *Relationships (love; home; partner; children; family; friends etc).*

• *Mind, Body, Spirit (personal growth; spiritual growth; health; exercise etc).*

• *Recreation (sport; social; travel etc).*

From previous exercises and reflection, you should already have a good idea of what your desires and needs are in each of the four main areas of life.

• *In each of the areas write your long-term goals.*

• *For each long-term goal write your short-term goals.*

• *For each short-term goal write some immediate steps you can take.*

• *Assign a time-frame to each of your goals — a date at which time you will arrive at each goal.*

• *Write down the benefits of achieving your short-term and long-term goals and the journey along the way.*

Example:

Long-term goal:
To become a Physiotherapist with my own practice 2010.

Short-term goals:
Save money for study Dec 2002
Start study with college/university Jan 2003
Complete study with college/university Dec 2006
Obtain a job as a Physiotherapist Jan 2007
Start my own practice Jan 2010.

Immediate Steps:
Enquire as to courses available
Put saving plan into place
Read books about subject
Do short course on "owning your own business"
Continue with self-awareness, affirmations and visualisations.

Benefits of Journey:
Increased self-worth and self-confidence
Courage to take further risks in future
Belief in self and abilities
Positive feelings of stimulation and challenge
Use my talents and expertise to help others
Freedom of doing what I love.

Reinforce your Goals

Reinforce your goals with the skills and tools you have learned:

- State your intention daily — "it is my intention to become a successful physiotherapist with my own thriving practice"

- Use affirmations to support you in obtaining your goals; changing beliefs which limit and discourage to beliefs which serve and encourage

- Use visualisations to see, feel and experience your desires with excitement and great joy

- Continue to build self-worth, self-esteem and self-confidence

- Connect to your Higher Self and Creative Source — your true nature is already loving, joyous, wise, creative and peaceful — find ways to remember who you are

- Cultivate gratitude consciousness for that which is, and that which is still to come

- Practice being in the present moment — the place of power and clarity — the place where future worries and past regrets do not exist.

Action

Without movement you are only potential — action brings potential into reality.

If you want to achieve your dreams and goals, you have to be willing to take action. You have to be willing to persevere and not give up when you experience a setback. You have to be willing to make a commitment to follow through. You have to have the courage to take risks and to leap into the unknown. Your positive actions reinforce your belief in yourself, which attracts further success.

Action is your demonstration of commitment to your dreams and goals. Until you are committed there is hesitancy and procrastination. Remind yourself of your goals and act on them everyday. Affirm daily, visualise and state your intention — draw opportunities to yourself.

Keep your motivation alive by focussing on the benefits of setting out on your journey and celebrate your successes along the way.

Acknowledge and Celebrate Your Success

Acknowledge and celebrate your successes — the big and small. Success isn't the accomplishment of your desires and goals. You are successful when you recognise your special talents; listen to your inner whisperings; transform a limiting belief into an empowering one; release a fear; choose to love yourself; act upon your desires; take risks; respect yourself and others; and make a contribution to others.

Success is a journey, not a destination. The only way to enjoy success is to learn to enjoy the process along the way — to enjoy what you are doing in the present moment.

Remember that goal setting is not a one-off exercise. As it is the nature of all life to evolve and grow, you will find new desires emerge as old desires are satisfied. At least every six months you should review your goals. Adjust those goals needing adjustment, and replace those which are achieved with new goals.

Key No 7
PERSEVERING AND REMAINING DETERMINED (YET FLEXIBLE)

"Failure is nothing but success trying to be born in a bigger way"

Catherine Ponder

Optimism and Perseverance

Persevering in the face of set-backs is vital to your experience of success and prosperity. Too often, people give up when the going gets tough. However, successful and prosperous people have a habit of persisting no matter how many obstacles or set-backs they experience.

To be able to persevere and persist, you need to have an optimistic attitude. Not a false optimism that denies the existence of obstacles and set-backs, but a "can do" attitude towards obstacles and set-backs. In every journey there will be obstacles — to think otherwise is setting yourself up for failure. The difference between people who succeed and people who fail is their attitude toward these obstacles and set-backs. People who have an optimistic attitude see obstacles as hurdles to be overcome, as challenges to be worked through. People who do not have an optimistic attitude see obstacles as brick walls preventing them from moving any further. Often they view setbacks as confirmation of a fatal flaw in themselves — they take everything personally. Do you see setbacks as confirming a fatal flaw in yourself that cannot be changed? Or do you see setbacks as things outside yourself which you are able to overcome and consequently build strength of character?

Your attitude toward obstacles and set-backs will determine your experience of success and prosperity. If you can view them as gifts that strengthen you and develop your potential then you will find perseverance comes more easily. If you can view them as "learning experiences", you can use what you learned to try something different. With an optimistic attitude, you experience every event on your journey as a help to developing the qualities, strengths and consciousness you need to attract success and prosperity.

Perseverance requires that you remain determined, yet flexible. You need to be flexible enough to know that there is no perfection or completion.

Faith, Trust and Expectation

When waiting for something to come, or if something hasn't manifested within the time frame you set, do not allow yourself to become discouraged. Have faith and trust you can have what you have requested — that your desires and goals already exist within you and will manifest at the right time. If you view your circumstances from a bigger perspective, it may be what is happening to you now, is preparing you for the future.

It may be that you need to grow and evolve in some way — change a limiting belief; have more self-worth; create more self-confidence. It may be that you need to let go of something. Trust that the obstacles, set-backs and challenges you experience on your journey assist you to do this. Trust that everything is laying the foundation for your good to manifest in the right way and at the right time.

When you disconnect from your trust in your own creative ability and from your trust in a friendly, cooperative universe, then you experience anxiety and worry. When you disconnect from your trust you become fearful and lose the expectation that your desires will manifest.

Expectation involves faith. If you are to manifest what you desire, you must have faith in your creative ability. You must have faith in the abundance and cooperativeness of the universe.

Patience

When you trust in your creative ability, you allow yourself the quality of patience. Impatience is a failure to trust in yourself, the process of life and the abundance of the universe.

When you find yourself trying to hurry or force a result, your thinking becomes fearful. As your reality is a product of your consciousness, you will create what you fear. All reality is a manifestation of love or its opposite — fear. When you create from fear you will always attract to yourself that which you do not want.

When you come from a place of trust and patience you are able to relinquish your attachment to your desire or goal.

Detachment

When you find yourself emotionally attached to your desire or goal, your thinking becomes fearful. You either fear not getting what you want; or fear the unknown. It is therefore necessary to relinquish your attachment to your desires and goals.

You are able to detach easily when you develop trust in yourself and the universe. Detachment is based on the unquestioning belief in your creative power and Creative Source. Relinquishing your attachment to your desires and goals is an internal act of faith; a willingness to let go of a particular outcome; knowing that success and prosperity will come. You retain your intention and your desire, but you give up your attachment to the result.

When you are attached to your desires and goals; when you feel your well-being is dependent upon having them, your neediness comes from fear. In fear you grasp for the known. What is the known? It is your comfort zone, your old patterns, your limiting beliefs. Therefore embrace uncertainty — uncertainty of the outcome — uncertainty of the result. Uncertainty is very different to doubt. Doubt is not believing your good will come, whereas uncertainty is simply not knowing how your good will come.

Letting go of your attachment symbolises your faith in your creative ability and in an abundant universe. Letting go opens you to infinite possibilities. The degree to which you are open is the degree to which miracles will happen. Let go and let God.

THE NEXT STEP
FROM CREATOR TO CO-CREATOR

*"There is one animating spiritual intelligence with infinitely
diverse expressions of itself.
Each of us is a living manifestation
of that intelligence — sacred, unique, precious and vital
to the evolution of the whole".*
Barbara Hubbard

Our personal and spiritual growth sets the stage for the awakening of "social growth" As we evolve individually, the level of consciousness on our planet also evolves. This occurs in response to the contribution of individuals who, as they evolve personally reflect their insights back to the society in which they live. Our first responsibility is to realise our own creative potential, and to then bring forth our creative potential into the world. We will then take the leap from the creator of our own reality, to co-creators with Universal Intelligence and with each other.

The profound problems of our time — individual, social, spiritual and global — are a reflection of our internal crises. Our loss of direction, loss of meaning, disconnection from the environment and the planet, mirror our disconnection from our Creative Source. The illusion of separateness we accept as our reality, mirrors our disconnection from our Higher Self. We have forgotten the deeper layer of experience we share with all creation, as we have lost connection with our Higher Self.

The challenges we face collectively — environmental degradation, resource depletion, injustice and inequality — have been a catalyst for an uprising of a new consciousness. This new consciousness is forcing us to embrace our interconnectedness, our oneness. It is laying the foundation for us to seek our uniqueness, not through separation and competition as in the past, but through cooperation and contribution to the whole.

In the current paradigm, where many of us still see ourselves as separate, we feel powerless to affect the whole and ask ourselves — "what difference can I possibly make?" In *The Rebirth of Nature* Rupert Sheldrake's 'morphic resonance' theory suggests that if one member of a species performs a certain behaviour, it affects all others ever so slightly, and if repeated frequently enough over sufficient time, its effects, builds up and begins to affect the entire species. It is in this way that paradigm shifts occur. Therefore, each individual makes a huge difference — the change in one facilitates the change in many. One individual committed to their higher vision is a powerful force in the universe.

We are now being called to take our place as co-creators in a much needed paradigm shift. We all have a part to play in co-creating a visionary new world. And it starts when we are courageous enough to connect with our Higher Self, listen to our inner wisdom, identify our life purpose and bring it forth into the world.

Recommended Reading

Bloch, Douglas
    Listen To Your Inner Voice 1991
    Hazelden Foundation

Branden, Nathaniel
    The Six Pillars Of Self-Esteem 1994
    Bantam Books

Chopra, Deepak
    The Seven Spiritual Laws Of Success 1994
    Bantam Press

Dyer, Wayne
    Manifest Your Destiny 1997
    HarperCollins Publishers

Edwards, Gill
    Living Magically 1991
    Judy Piatkus (Publishers) Ltd

Gawain, Shakti
    Creative Visualisation 1978
    Whatever Publishing

Gawain, Shakti
    Creating True Prosperity 1997
    New World Library

Genders, Lyn
    First Steps To Meditation 1999
    Axiom Publishing

Goleman, Daniel
    Emotional Intelligence 1995
    Bloomsbury Publishing

Gray, John
    How To Get What You Want
    & Want What You Have 1999
    Pan Macmillan Aust Pty Ltd

Hanna, Paul
>   *Believe & Achieve* 1998
>   Penguin Books Aust Ltd

Hay, Louise L.
>   *You Can Heal Your Life* 1999
>   Hay House Inc

Hubbard, Barbara
>   *Conscious Evolution* 1998
>   New World Library

Jeffers, Susan
>   *Feel The Fear And Do It Anyway* 1987
>   Arrow Books Ltd

McGraw, Phillip
>   *Life Strategies* 1999
>   Random House Aust (Pty) Ltd

Millman, Dan
>   *The Law Of Spirit:*
>   *Truths For Making Life Work* 1995
>   H.J. Kramer Inc

Moore, Thomas
>   *Care Of The Soul A Guide For Cultivating Depth*
>   *& Sacredness In Everyday Life* 1992
>   HarperCollins Publishers Inc

Morris, Tom
>   *True Success* 1994
>   Judy Piatkus (Publishers) Ltd

Ponder, Catherine
>   *The Dynamic Laws Of Prosperity* 1962
>   DeVorss & Co

Rowland, Michael
>   *Absolute Happiness* 1993
>   Self Communications Pty Ltd